LEGIBLE WALLS

LEGIBLE WALLS
Copyright © 2023 by Darryl Lorenzo Wellington
ISBN: 978-1-7369128-8-1

First paperback edition published by Stalking Horse Press, June 2023

All rights reserved. Except for brief passages quoted for review or academic purposes, no part of this book may be reproduced, stored in a retrieval system, or transmitted by any means without the written permission of the author and publisher. Published in the United States by Stalking Horse Press.

Publishing Editor: James Reich
Design by James Reich

Stalking Horse Press
Santa Fe, New Mexico

www.stalkinghorsepress.com

DARRYL LORENZO WELLINGTON

LEGIBLE WALLS

POEMS FOR SANTA FE MURALS

STALKING HORSE PRESS
SANTA FE, NEW MEXICO

CONTENTS

Untitled — 9
Mirages — 10
Proem — 11
Lamp-lit — 15
Lady of Justice — 17
Lady of Sweeter Justice — 18
The First Image is Public Art — 20
A Creative Writing Exercise — 22
The Flâneur and the Neighborhood Mural — 25
Excerpt from "Days of Protest"— 33
La Ronde — 37
The Last Snowfall in New Mexico — 41
The Next Town — 52

ACKNOWLEDGMENTS

Some of these poems previously appeared in the collection, *Psalms at the Present Time*.

The photographs in the book were provided by:
Matthew Chase-Daniel
Ronnie Ortiz
Fatima Van Hattum
and The City of Santa Fe Arts Commission.

To magicians, mavericks and muralists.

*Thanks also to the City of Santa Fe Arts Commission
for supporting this project.*

children come and go
residents bleed and die houses
slump
totter neighborhoods
decay
renew   resuscitate
gentrify. Walls remain.
Paint the walls.

Paint the walls
the stories
you only recognize
from having heard them iterated
too often
to segregate the primary secondary the penumbra images in a dream:
mnemonic memory
paper   scissors   rock
the ABCs.

MIRAGES

I see mirages—my books, that is, generally speaking begin with collections of riddles, tiny insidious lights, mysterious UFOs and mirages that beckon me. After I became the Santa Fe Poet Laureate 2021-2023, I crisscrossed the city bringing my lessons to public and private schools and schoolchildren. Then I retraced my routes bringing the poems they had written back home. I visited sections of the city I had never visited before, and along the way—whether to success, failure, or poetry and play—painted walls beckoned me…

PROEM

Look at a large, multi-paneled street mural in an urban setting. Give it a lingering gaze. You will start to realize it isn't an illustration of a public space. It's a sensory mirror. And the saying so goes too that if you stare into any mirror long enough—until the evening light brandishes the coming moonlight—the reflection changes. Finds new visages. New perspectives. A mural will recast a block, a neighborhood—invert its symbols inside and out—like a history without borders.

Yes, I have lived in cities that were famous for secret alleys and gardens. Gardens that you wouldn't believe existed, except if you were invited inside special gates. Santa Fe is no less mysterious than those other places, because the city harbors close to secluded neighborhoods, invisible until you leave your car and turn a corner. The accidental visitor time travels, down exquisitely narrow streets, back to precious adobe houses, small windows, back to burros leaving dust tracks. Embarrassments of riches. I felt enchanted and estranged. The "old school" neighborhoods that I have stumbled upon exude privileged mystery. The neighborhoods have granted me a temporary permission slip. One side reads *Welcome;* the other reads, *Invitation Only.*

...

Find a mural. Appreciate its thesis/antithesis. Drink its revolution. It dignifies an intended public space. You cannot encounter a mirror—an authentic mirror—by *Invitation Only*.

Regardless of the location a public mural is a sigh of relief. Say, an image may be inconspicuous—hidden in a corner that's infrequently seen or covered with shrubbery; still by virtue of *street life* no one is estranged. No one is disallowed. You have encountered a flag for a country without citizenship papers.

Its presence asks for a token payment or show of appreciation with a stare, a gasp, a chuckle, a measurable indication of surprise. Its visual language may be political, cultural, comical, shocking, or criminal. Sequentially matters, creates momentum, but no sequentially contains all that matters. The language is vertiginous. The reason wall art is garish, bright, loud, or tasteless is so that you can't walk past without stumbling—or relinquishing resistance—before entering inside it.

For several months in 2021-2022, this piece of public "word art" created by Matthew Chase-Daniel and his assistants occupied a wall at the corner of Lena and Second Street, puzzling viewers on their way.

The sentences are lines isolated from my short poem "Lamp-Lit." The entirety of the poem was printed on the upper right hand corner of the wall. The wall however was more conveniently located for driving past than reading the small text.

The majority of observers inside their moving vehicles glimpsed and hopefully contemplated the enigmatic opening.

What is happening? A moth is circling a lamp, and its motion casts a roving shadow. The shadow is a flickering representation. A distortion. A recreation. But why call a representation an absence?

Throughout the work and domestic life you will pass by signs and mirrors and reflections and find yourself reflected in innumerable ways in other eyes and ears.

The representation of your world is not your world, even when you are included in the picture. The moth's furriness is not the shadow's blurriness.

But this is the best the world can offer. Why call a representation an absence?

LAMP-LIT

The moth casts a giant presence,
        —why call its shadow an absence?
formlessness,
loneliness,
like a pockmarked
hole widening an opening
into space, time, space, place,
of course, and time's eclipse
implied by the shape

that's flung
against a wall. This desert island-like *en masse* blear—
like an ink stain against the wall's calligraphy.
Accept that this is not an absence
Accept that this is a presence
Accept that the lividly solitary presence
may change moment to moment
indefinitely left behind by light's absence.

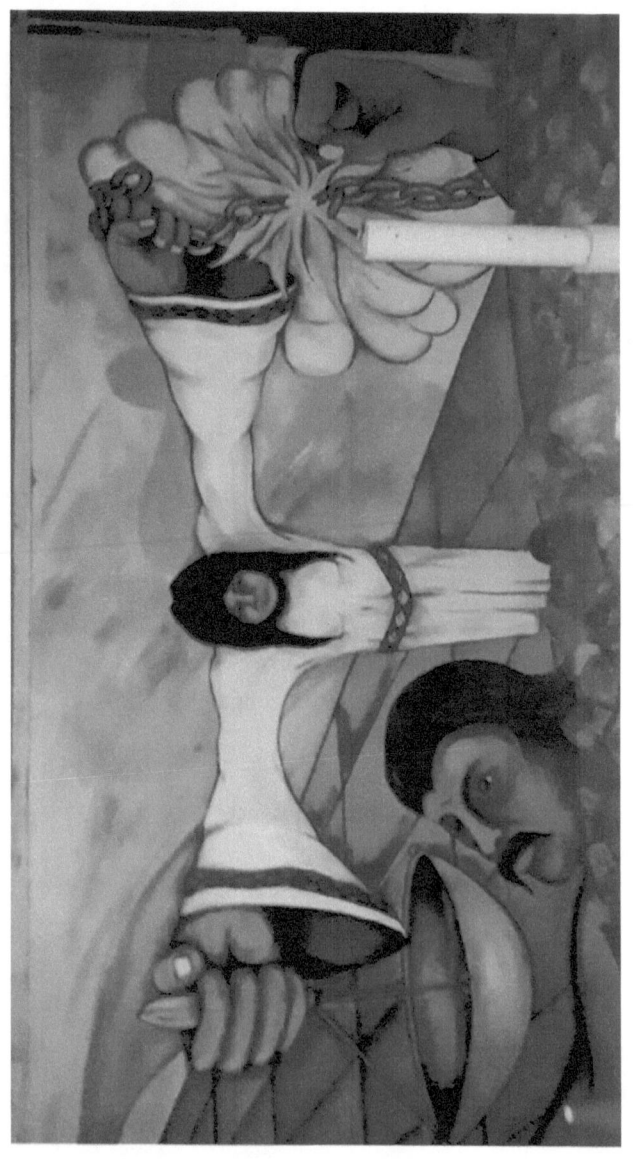

LADY OF JUSTICE

If you're looking for this image (and I advise you to go and give it deserved appreciation) you'll find it in a parking lot on Canyon Road. The image is painted on a nondescript stone edifice, like a centerpiece or an altar incongruously erected there. In my imagination the undistinguished block of stone exists for the sake of providing a masterpiece with a canvas.

Honors for the mural belong to artist Sam Leyba and his co-creators who executed a remarkable number of public murals in Santa Fe in the early 1970s, during a time of an upsurge in community activism, heavily inspired by the actions of AIM and the Brown Berets.

The imagery crackles with energy and ascent and assent.

The chains break…

The sleepers wake…

A proposed ascent—offered by the Lady of Sweeter Justice—may come any second. It comes in the middle of the night. It must first receive fervent worldly assent.

I approach the image synesthetically and hear wheels grinding, oppressive gravity leavening, and a monumental moment of historical momentum meeting less resistance… when a revolutionary Ascent is on the brink of Assent…

LADY OF SWEETER JUSTICE

The thumbs turned. The fists gripped.
The sky blanched. The chains kindled.
The links severed. When the aroma
dazzled the expectant workers, dazed
sandaled checkers at retail shopping centers,
stunned the noses of horticulturalists
who presumed a fertile and overzealous
spring mischievously excited local color
schemes crying *if this sweet oil exists,*
peace, justice and spirit was an opiate.

And looking back on it, all
the sighs of *Amen* and *ahem*
from the distance of many eons
with the impartiality of a scholar,
no one honestly suspected,
nobody knew to agree
before the turn of North winds South,
and the white robes billowing, a shaky
pan splashed distilled perfumes,
before the gardeners lightly, whimsically,
lifted blank gazes and smiled, *given this,*
peace, justice and spirit was an opiate.

Lucky you. You meet your first target. And arrive safely in an unfamiliar place. Your point of entry is the outskirts of town—counties of countless debris—where train tracks and overpasses and warehouses and graffiti proliferate...

THE FIRST IMAGE IS PUBLIC ART

From the first moments,
entering into an unmapped space
whether as humble as a 500 ft rental, or
vast as an aerial view's three dimensional cityscape
you'll recognize whether an aspect is emergent:
whether the image ensconced on the first billboard sign
                is emergent,
                    primary, incontestable,
whether it defines the commemoration of pedestrian
                    firstness as no imitation can
because the speed of recognition is immeasurably
                                  now.

Then as you enter the scene expectantly
        —high on the light rails—
                catch a sudden hint the vision is illicit and
Edenic
its firstness somehow lawlessly skewed,
or wrong and right—
and the part that is wrong defies ordinary
propriety, and worse,
the giveaway is that the signage stretches a length
that should be reserved for corporate logos or public policy

statements while this is salacious. You see a Yin/Yang symbol
until at the tail end
it becomes a coral snake. The fascination is virginal

                                          surrealist.

A CREATIVE WRITING EXERCISE

Creativity consists of describing what is, and imagining what possibly could be. The possibilities inspire imaginative excess. One of my favorite writing exercises was for a theater class where we wrote a one act play which could not be produced. Similarly, a painter, art critic or poet can describe and envision a hypothetical mural.

Could it exist? Is it an impossibility? Why?

What is its theme? Is it based on an alternative history?

Where is it located? And who lives and dies in this imaginary city? Who understands this narrative? Who is comfortable, or uncomfortably disposed?

And most importantly if you try this exercise convey the information in a way that describes what the mural looks like.

For example imagine the mural displays three images: paper, scissors, and rock

paper covers rock
        rock smashes scissors
                scissors cut paper

That's what they signify in this reality. Play with an imaginary alternative state, society, or future. Pretend these images carry a different meaning, or only a ghost of their past association with a child's game. Now write a poem from the perspective of their new meanings.

"Flâneur" is a French word which literally means "stroller" but connotes someone who wanders with an air of detachment, and a little bit "above it all." This person is an idler, an aesthete, and someone with an eye for restaurants and shops and paintings. This character believes their taste is culturally diverse. The flâneur wanders from gallery to gallery, studying the latest trends. Their cosmopolitanism is limited to gallery art they buy, sell, or trade. They meet a dilemma.

THE FLÂNEUR AND THE NEIGHBORHOOD MURAL

Here he comes. Why is he always chuckling? Who wanders without reference points? Who wanders without markers? Like a rambler in the valley of shades? Like a wise man, dispersing the last lamp light, too occasionally? Why is his intermittent silence, sound, or fury, firefly-like?

Too often, he admits, how many times past
he has given away his favorite clothes,
including finely tailored suits, rare books, collectables,
for no apparent reason, total impetuousness,
confusing them with shelf possessions,
like a child mistaking his lessons.

Is his courage really his cowardice?
Who gives away precious mementos
objects he loves, likes, relishes,
sometimes subversively,
self-consciously, impetuously,
sometimes intentionally to people he can barely stand?

He gifts away his bright prisms,
sea glass blazoning on his morning study,
at the hour when bluish-greenish refractions intensify.
They burn. They glow. They will have to go.
Give him his due. He has a deft plan. ...

Trapped in his psychological coils,
his past obsession has actually been
any chance to throw away cool gems,
leaving valuables in the surprised hands
of similarly self-possessed characters and

other charlatans he then shrugs aside.
Neighbors he couldn't call friends (or wouldn't).
Personalities he struggles to halfheartedly stomach.
He hands away his coolness like confetti.
Is this evidence of his lack of monetary attachments?
Or his set of curiously narcissistic repressions?

He represses his *wanderlust,* if anything.
His terror of being caught in just one place.
The flaneur distrusts the known.
Yet gives himself over to the unknown.
He is easily convinced he is someplace important
that is, if he can't identify where he is.

His heart is sentimental. He believes
his peripatetic behavior is evidentiary,
his nonchalant morality is charitable,
like counterbalancing weights.
Catch him here. Catch him over there.

Catch him clumsily misdirected and
bumping into an inconvenient lamppost.
He is probably not lost, just the sort who
is a wavering moth to a flame and

if he was accosted with criminal or noncriminal intent,
before he was told, would shortly empty his pockets.

⋮

Who can walk past

Triton's tributaries

Neptune-colored walls   brightness
      gestapo-garish

not laughing

not stumbling   skipping steps

confusing his balance   stumbling

in synesthesia

who blows smoke rings

   like nominal laser beams

      prismatic blasts

pulverizing the pedestrian

who takes for granted
objects of beauty, like shelf mementos

       ...

who ignores the imagery above below vertical and
horizontal and sky and sidewalk and yet
the mural opens
up like the horizon in April.

⁞

A painted wall indistinguishable from the elements? Analogous to sea, sky, or fire, too, how can he own it? Or barter it? Or gift it?

Where is left, right, center,
if the sight-seer is on the street,

and where is eye level,
if the aesthete is *en plein air*?

Where is his pedestrian
understanding, as
he runs smack into his
clumsy being, like a different person? Now that he knows a mural is a public mirror, let him make up his mind. And the saying so goes that he will see what he wants to see, and see what he can't afford to have seen, turning loose pages of neighborhood history.

DEFUND THE POLICE
SAY HER NAME
NO JUSTICE NO PEACE
NO RACIST POLICE
BLM
SOLIDARITY
BLACK LIVES ARE SACRED

One of my favorite "legible walls" in Santa Fe was created sometime in 2020 during the national protests over the execution of George Floyd, murdered by the police officer, Derek Chauvin. Marches and vigils erupted across America, including Santa Fe. A commemorative mural proclaiming "Black Lives Matter" was visibly displayed in the Railyard district. It made a powerful statement—a multi-paneled piece of work, evoking an aesthetic where mural-making meets collage.

The collective effort is credited to: Abdul Aziz, Devin J. Baldwin, Anne Stavely, Israel Haros Lopez, Taslim van Hattum, Fatima van Hattum, Samia van Hattum, Sean Clark, Dominique Butler, and Autumn Gomez.

The complete BLM mural no longer exists. It was eventually dismantled, but signs created by the same collaborative were relocated to two homes, until they were defaced in late October.

Santa Fe poet Fatima Van Hattum remembers that her sister Taslim "coordinated, curated, and compiled everyone's art for the mural and led us with the wheat pasting. Each individual plywood panel was hung as a community effort with a larger group of people.

"We also created similar smaller wheat paste BLM signs that were hung all over Santa Fe, including on the fence in front of my home and the fence in front of Samia's home. The signs were defaced at both of our homes. They also broke the back windshields on both Samia and my cars."

Murals come and go. They are well-protected, marginally protected, or unprotected. They are ravaged by wind, rain and elements. They are torn down, or painted over at the whims of building owners. Perhaps a landlord commissioned the work, but a new landlord expunges it. Or perhaps—like in 2020—a mural is wrecked by retaliatory vandalism, smeared over with red paint?

Times have tempered since the police office Derek Chauvin was convicted for murdering George Floyd. His conviction calmed the manifold expressions of grief and indignation, like the BLM street art that proliferated when concerned citizens and youth across the county untied behind a necessary statement. The relationship is unmistakable between the need to "hit the streets" and paint the streets in blazoning glory.

I can safely say that movements and murals rise and fall with national swells. But coming and going is not their untimely end. Protests that have riveted the nation so powerfully as BLM did in the 2020—when the movement transformed the national dialogue around race and police misconduct—cannot ever become irrelevant. They have become a part of American history. They have a revolutionary consciousness that haunts the nation. They come, they go, and— when their revolutionary message is required—they revive. And murals? Can they linger, like ghosts?

I wrote a poem in 2020 "Days of Protest" that, looking back, speaks of an unstoppable "eternal succession." BLM's inevitability is also the theme in "La Ronde." There will always be committed activists who stand ready to hit the streets. Imagine that the refrain "We will not disappear" extends to the movement, the imagery, even the murals.

EXCERPT FROM "DAYS OF PROTEST"

We will smash the world
Wildly
We will thunder…
Roses and dreams
Debased by poets
Will unfurl…
   —*The 150.000.000, Mayakovski*

We will not disappear.
like her birth name
like his dead letters
buried inside a sheaf
after a flash rain …

We will not disappear.

⋮

Death yawns stately.
Death conjoins us.
—whether we make music
noise, love, or bourgeoisie war.
Free assembly and funeral
rites, these days, symbiotic, interchangeable.

Siren sounds. We will not disappear

⁞

      we proceed like marionettes
carried along on one string
crowds of selfsame mouths
our tongues chant now in unison
the pitch like a cracked accordion
then canticle is cant
and cry.
              and the dead also
They will not disappear.

⁞

Death conjoins us. The streets
indigenously compel us
whether we lay down
and recharge
screaming at planned events
protests marches
and vigils
have become
intermarried, like a sexual transgression

Death conjoins us

⁞

Death pulls back the curtain.

Public war,
like private mourning,
pulls back the curtain.
An old law is a heavy sigh.
Its retellings, latchkey shibboleth   *blood nurses grief,*
grief nurses war,

and what else is changed to soldiers and mourners?

⸸

We wear hoodies and chains

—hoodies, sneakers, jerseys, chains;
 lining the streets carrying placards,
 banners
 and loudspeakers
 amplifying   *Trayvon   Breonna*
                EricGarnerFreddieGreyPhilandoCastle
    like aggravated parlor ghosts
 And sound systems reify the abstractions:
 let the crowds inspire regardless
 belief in eternal succession…

LA RONDE

Everything that you have at stake is just a *pittance*.
A *pittance?*—such is the designation of cheap goods, wools
bundled up at embarrassing rates, Lordy Lord, Lord,
such is the destination of unworn materials
sold at pennies per yard. Per yard? Per line, per loss.
Per regards survival at the fittest. Clotho's
implacable line, listen, is too rich for your blood anyway
and unspools in tricolors. Alongside her competitive
and wickedly thonged Olympian sisters. Sibling-soldiers? Thighs
bulging like strapped-on muscles. Whose competitive plan is
ferocious? Victorious. Whose thread is an off-shoot of dank
yellow cloudily silvered? Everything at stake. While listening—
pedals insidiously whistling—watch their sandaled feet.
Clotho's toe polish is hot lava scarlet; Lachesis prefers
Fifth Avenue blue. Blue-toned *Bustling Bazaar*. And Atropos, the
bulkiest woman-warrior sibling severs the threads—
her jowls bulging, her short, matted hair topped
and split like a rooster's wet crown, invariably, lazily,
hazily paints her 10 pusillanimous piggies
crayon-colors sparkling like flint, the terrific kick-ass
hues for going full-out to town, *Shadows of the Gods,* of course,
*China Glaze Halloween Lacquer Black, Pining for You
Black.* The race is on. Race? Which race? Whose loom

...

spins the threads of Anglo/White/Black/Asian/Indigenous
historical oppression? Who threads the classic line, *Black
Lives Matter*? And which spinner promises oppositional
othered minority identities their sudden death? *'Tis a*
pity.
Note: these three super-human stallions breakneck
mortally unassailable deities wear pairs of $600 sandals
per regards life, loss, longing, purposelessness
—in particular since lesser mortals who won't escape
world-weariness anyway can't make much of a scandal—
but all that the Olympian spinners Clotho Lachesis Atropos
—'tis a pity—
have at stake is *a pittance* beneath their heels

The *Alas De Aqua Collective's* "Water is Life" mural at the Salvador Perez recreation center is a powerfully synesthetic artistic experience that surrounds an indoor pool. The imagery is a meditation on the philosophical and material significance of water throughout the human cycle of life and death. The space is simultaneously a physical, a visual, and an imaginative enchantment.

As I wandered the space 'checking it out' (but only halfway enjoying the whole experience because I wasn't swimming) a lifeguard approached me inquiringly. When told him I was impressed with the art. "Sure is better than looking at bare walls" he responded.

The panels belong to various *Alas De Agua* artists. Several panels emphasize the miraculous. Water is divine. In a poetic sense just a droplet—a water seed—can begin the process that culminates in renewal. John-Paul Granillo wrote that his painting of a mystical seed highlighted "how little water is used by a cactus to survive in such harsh conditions. Like the cactus, the people of New Mexico need to keep a drop of hope to survive before the night falls. In current times, we are living with the fear of Covid-19, and social injustice becoming a normality. We have large amounts of pressure to deal with, as a nation, as a family unit, and as individuals. My dream is that we can be bold like that drop of water, and continue to hold on to our hope."

THE LAST SNOWFALL IN NEW MEXICO

The future is hypothetical—its providence is hypothetical—but each passing season is tangible. Spring, winter, summer, and autumn is material; the shape of green leaves bursting on the trees is ineluctable; sap's smell is inescapable. However indefinable they may be, snow, sleet and rain still soothe, or sting, or prick the flesh. In this vision of a terrifying post-apocalypse, in this viscerally unhappy future, snowfall has strangely become a rarity. Snow. Callen has never seen it. He misunderstands it. His ignorance is such he doesn't realize to touch it is more significant than to just see it. In a sense, some say, because his generation has rarely touched it a bond has been broken, or the union of the intangible and the material, like the marriage of hope and dreams has been severed. The right conditions have become sadly, sadly uncommon.

...

⁞

Callen knows it may come briefly, furtive, frazzled snow, sometimes here in the Southwest, collapsing too lightly to merit poetry. But a material element as well as an immaterial element in dreams has disappeared, sacrificed to a blistering sun that punishes the scorched earth. He has been told there was a time before the sun shriveled, like a dwarf planet, a dust mote inside a shaded bulb. The sun was ironically massive. And colder and crueler. There was a time when snowfall blanketed continents. Branches bowed, weighted under whiteness. Sleet crushed walls. Winds deposited ice. Trees sank into the ground as heavily as desecrated sheep. Buildings tottered beneath blizzards. An ice storm was regular. Snowfall was constant. But since then, troubled, strangled, evanescent. Its memory is precious, fetishized, like distantly shimmering jewelry. Revisiting its memory, which is a hungry, nostalgic memory for the slushy white plains, old people pretend they can finger it. It consists of small particles, it dissolves, it is as striking as *evanescent*. Yet while they provide "the big picture" no one can tell him. How long since last snowfall in New Mexico?

⋮

Callen squeezes the dreadful head.
Turns. Turns. Twists the spigot,
droplets occur,
reoccurrence reestablishes safety, security, belief,
and he wonders whether the familiar taste faintly
resembles
the other stuff,
snow,
but snow resembles creamier water.
Sweetened. No. Scarcity is never sweet.

...

⋮

Callen suffocates, if he fantasizes too long about what life was like, before the kindling. The kindling? The new world is as parched as a wound with too little water to make a salve. New Mexico drought makes everything crackle. Sidewalks sting. Bodies wrinkle. Sap seeps. Fabrics crackle. His hair burns, his body is less like a host of sensations than a night wind that steals moisture. He wants to strip his clothes, yet he still itches and scratches when naked.

...

⋮

before the pipe spurts,

tinnily, the faucet whirs—

the music is thin, metallic, mechanical, atonal, like the faucet

has a seed stuck in its throat: but a water droplet

is not a knot of hair

is not a piece of stick

is not a non-biodegradable element that clogs

the drainage systems

if a water droplet is formidable and fruitful

if a water droplet is invidious and implosive

if a water droplet is miraculous and destructive it is—

      —synonymously—

Atomic.

⋮

Evanescence. Evanescence. Whispers the word, haunted by it. As ghostly sounding as how its definitions, its syllables trip and turn, or threaten to erupt at the apex of his frustration. *To be evanescent,* Callen thinks, must mean to survive nearer an end point. Nothing is permanent. How apropos could any other word be compared to its sibilance that leaves Callen's tongue heat exhausted and smarting? He realizes at sixteen that his world is a chancy business. He is too hot to read, too thirsty to sleep; sometimes, restless, he shuts himself behind closed doors. And in his erotized sickness, rather than flesh, he sometimes pictures snow. He struggles to focus in school. The other kids struggle, no less, because they have been deflated body and soul. They hurry home, panting in the blistering heat. They rarely learn their lessons. It is too much to ask because the pages tatter. The print frays. The computers screens discolor, going fuzzy. The high school administrators freely declare that in the coming weeks school closes early, or closes five days straight, admitting the enterprise is hard to maintain. The world after all is as brittle as a dry forest. Ready for kindling. School learning and book learning is as valueless nowadays as a primitive toy that has been brutalized until it risks falling apart. Nobody cares much, neither parents, teachers, students, nor neighbors, penitents themselves, wiry survivors of a scorched earth.

...

§

He hears his friends ask, *Will there be water soon? How about rain?*

He hears his parents ask, *How much longer can we live with uncertainty and evanescence?*

He asks himself, *How long since the last snowfall in New Mexico?*

Mural-making is known for being 'gaudy' depending upon one's taste. But the most 'gaudy' mural in Santa Fe—again depending upon one's taste—isn't on a wall.

The Santa Fe Sky Railway Line that makes treks between Santa Fe and Lamy is the brainchild of *Game of Thrones* novelist George R. R. Martin, who purchased the historic line in 2021, refurbished interiors which dated back to the 1920s, and transformed the line into a fantasy adventure ride. George R. R. Martin has explained that "Sky Railway adventures are one-of-a-kind immersive experiences, and we're teeming with ideas for all sorts of exciting outings," featuring live music, cocktails, and immersive mystery theater. The "trip" is not between points A and B. It's a "trip" in the slangy sense of an unpredictable and unbelievable adventure.

To enhance the getaway narrative, George R. R. Martin commissioned muralist Joerael Numina. An article in *Travel and Leisure* magazine lauded Numina's murals. "While train operators have traditionally regarded graffiti artists as nuisances, Sky Railway is embracing the art form, with one painted as a dragon and the other a wolf." A glossily fanged dragon writhes across an unmistakable Sky Train—that much I easily remember—dovetailing with a general impression of outrageous party colors. Is it glaringly gross? Or is it an invitation to a fantasy release? If you don't like it, or point a rude finger at it, then you believe the garishness is over-the-top.

Thumbs Up or Thumbs Down is not my point.
Approval or disapproval is less important than getting on board an imaginary excursion. Where are you going? I am always—in my train dreams—returning to the coastal South. Where are you headed in a make-believe extravaganza? Where is the next town?

THE NEXT TOWN

[for the brightly illustrated Sky Railway Cars]

Spring weather raises
my blood pressure
like an emergency.

⁞

cacophonic colors make
any place revolutionary
enter at your own risk
if the train is topped
with fiery dragon

scales, mammalian fins,
murky metamorphoses,
pull the curtains and
leave at earliest convenience

Expect a fantasy adventure
unprecedented in the known world of crayons.

Murky metamorphoses make tinctures
whose depths gush like oil fields—

Plan another getaway
from this getaway
where the colors have less glare.

Catch your breath
in a forever-summer town, or
catch your death in wintry states instead.

⋮

I rise toward horizons
look down (from not
so very distantly) at the shining sea
blue waves, scarlet shore
unraveling like a thousand flags American.

Going to Savannah, Charleston,
chugalugging thataway
beneath an Eastern Sky Ocean
the train passes red clay hills
larger than festive April giants.

Through the window glass—
rain-soaked trees lean heavily
like fallen shoulders.

Dreams of a weird place—
Towers of glass and vacant clouds;
mouths without faces.

...

Spring smells like a new
perfume in a green bottle:
nature's best season.

A BIOGRAPHY

Darryl Lorenzo Wellington was the 6th Poet Laureate of Santa Fe, New Mexico, who served during 2021-2023.

During his tenure he visited dozens of schools, civic organizations, educational facilities, historical societies, and taught numerous workshops, often emphasizing the importance of confronting racism, social injustice, economic disparity, and historical legacies of oppression.

Born in Savannah, Georgia, and subsequently a long-time resident of Charleston, South Carolina, before relocating Southwest in 2010, he is an eclectic poet, journalist, and syndicated columnist with over twenty years of experience publishing commentary in publications, including *Dissent, The Nation, The Progressive, The Washington Post, Art Papers, The Santa Fe Reporter, The Crisis* (*The NAACP magazine*), *The Christian Science Monitor, The Common Review, Boston Review, ABZ Magazine, Drum Voices, The Journal of Blacks in Higher Education, The Guardian, Talk Poverty,* and *N+1*.

His best-known investigative journalism includes "New Orleans: A Right to Return" (*Dissent magazine*) a lengthy exploration of repatriation issues following Hurricane Katrina, "The Twisted Business of Donating Plasma" (*The Atlantic*) an expose of the plasma industry and "Reality Publishing" (*N+1 magazine*).

a philosophical reexamination of the Amazon publishing phenomenon. He recently published "The Beloved Community: Danny Lyon's Photographs during the Civil Rights Era" inside the catalogue for photographer Danny Lyon's retrospective at the Albuquerque Museum of Art.

His poetry chapbook *Life's Prisoners* received the 2017 Turtle Island Quarterly Chapbook Award. His first full-length collection is *Psalms for the Present Time* (Flowstone Press, 2021). His poetry has been anthologized in *In Fullness of the Word: an anthology of Black American Poet Laureates,* published by 5th Woman Books.

Wellington is a public speaker who has appeared on the *Tavis Smiley Radio Show,* and *Democracy Now.* He is also a performance artist, best known for historical reenactments in which he portrays Richard Wright, the author of *Native Son.* These presentations reintroduce contemporary audiences to the life and times of the first Black American to publish a bestseller, overtly criticizing white supremacy.

Whenever he is asked which medium he prefers. Wellington answers that in his poetry or performance, his nonfiction, or his public speaking, he returns to the theme of social justice. In life, as well as art, he loves playing with fire.

www.ingramcontent.com/pod-product-compliance
Lightning Source LLC
Chambersburg PA
CBHW021135080526
44587CB00012B/1309